YEAR-ROUND FAVORITES

HAWAIIAN BREAD FRENCH TOAST	4
CRANBERRY ORANGE SCONES	6
OVERNIGHT BACON, SOURDOUGH, EGG AND CHEESE CASSEROLE	8
CORN CHIP CHILI	10
BROCCOLI CHEDDAR SOUP	12
MEATBALLS AND SPAGHETTI SAUCE	14
SLOW-COOKED SHAKSHUKA	16
HEARTY VEGETARIAN MAC AND CHEESE	18
CHILE RELLEÑOS	20
STEAMED AFRICAN CORN LOAF	22
COLCANNON	24
TWICE "BAKED" POTATOES	26
ROCKY ROAD BROWNIE BOTTOMS	28
CINNAMON ROLL-TOPPED MIXED BERRY COBBLER	30

HAWAIIAN BREAD FRENCH TOAST

MAKES 8 TO 10 SERVINGS

- 6 eggs
- 1 cup milk
- 1 cup whipping cream
- 2 teaspoons coconut extract
- 2 teaspoons vanilla
- 1 teaspoon ground cinnamon
- ¼ cup sugar
- 1 pound sliced sweet Hawaiian rolls or bread, sliced lengthwise and cut to fit CROCK-POT® slow cooker
- 2 tablespoons unsalted butter, cut into ¼-inch pieces
- ½ cup flaked coconut, toasted*

*To toast coconut, spread in single layer in heavy-bottomed skillet. Cook and stir over medium heat 1 to 2 minutes until lightly browned. Remove from skillet immediately. Cool before using.

1. Coat inside of **CROCK-POT**® slow cooker with nonstick cooking spray. Whisk eggs, milk, cream, coconut extract, vanilla, cinnamon and sugar in large bowl.

2. Place bread in **CROCK-POT**® slow cooker; sprinkle butter over top. Pour egg mixture on top; press bread down to absorb egg mixture. Cover; cook on HIGH 2 hours. Sprinkle with toasted coconut.

CRANBERRY ORANGE SCONES

MAKES 6 SERVINGS

- ¼ cup (½ stick) cold butter
- 1 cup plus 2 tablespoons self-rising flour, divided
- ¾ cup buttermilk
- 2 teaspoons granulated sugar
- ¼ cup dried cranberries
- 1½ teaspoons orange peel, divided
- ½ teaspoon ground cinnamon
- ¼ cup powdered sugar
- 1½ teaspoons orange juice
- ⅛ teaspoon salt

1. Cut one 16-inch piece of parchment paper; fold in half crosswise. Fit parchment paper into bottom and partly up sides of 1½-quart **CROCK-POT**® slow cooker. Coat parchment paper with nonstick cooking spray.

2. Grate cold butter into medium bowl. Add 1 cup flour, buttermilk and granulated sugar; stir until dry ingredients are just moistened. *Do not overmix.* Combine cranberries, 1 teaspoon orange peel and cinnamon in small bowl; toss to coat. Fold cranberry mixture into dough.

3. Sprinkle work surface with remaining 2 tablespoons flour. Place dough on work surface; knead briefly until dough forms a ball. Press into 6-inch disc; score into six wedges. Place disc into **CROCK-POT**® slow cooker on top of parchment paper.

4. Lay clean kitchen towel across top of **CROCK-POT**® slow cooker; cover with lid. Cover; cook on HIGH 1½ hours. Remove scones with parchment paper to wire rack. Combine powdered sugar, orange juice, remaining ½ teaspoon orange peel and salt in small bowl; whisk until blended. Drizzle over scones; serve warm or at room temperature.

OVERNIGHT BACON, SOURDOUGH, EGG AND CHEESE CASSEROLE

MAKES 6 SERVINGS

- 1 loaf (about 12 ounces) sourdough bread, cut into ¾-inch cubes
- 8 slices thick-cut bacon, chopped
- 1 large onion, chopped
- 1 medium red bell pepper, chopped
- 1 medium green bell pepper, chopped
- 2 teaspoons dried oregano
- ¼ cup sun-dried tomatoes packed in oil, drained and chopped
- 1½ cups (6 ounces) shredded sharp Cheddar cheese, divided
- 10 eggs
- 1 cup milk
- 1 teaspoon salt
- ¾ teaspoon black pepper

1. Coat inside of **CROCK-POT**® slow cooker with nonstick cooking spray. Place bread in **CROCK-POT**® slow cooker. Heat large skillet over medium heat. Add bacon; cook 7 to 9 minutes or until crisp. Remove bacon to paper towel-lined plate, using slotted spoon. Pour off all but 1 tablespoon of drippings from skillet. Heat same skillet over medium heat. Add onion, bell peppers and oregano; cook 2 to 3 minutes or until onion is softened, stirring occasionally. Stir in sun-dried tomatoes; cook 1 minute. Pour over bread in **CROCK-POT**® slow cooker. Stir in bacon and 1 cup cheese.

2. Beat eggs, milk, salt and black pepper in large bowl; pour over bread mixture in **CROCK-POT**® slow cooker. Press down on bread to allow bread mixture to absorb egg mixture. Sprinkle remaining ½ cup cheese over top. Cover; cook on LOW 6 to 8 hours or on HIGH 3 to 4 hours. Cut into wedges to serve.

CORN CHIP CHILI

MAKES 6 SERVINGS

- 1 tablespoon olive oil
- 1 medium onion, chopped
- 1 medium red bell pepper, chopped
- 1 jalapeño pepper, seeded and finely chopped*
- 4 cloves garlic, minced
- 2 pounds ground beef
- 1 can (4 ounces) diced mild green chiles, drained
- 2 cans (about 14 ounces *each*) fire-roasted diced tomatoes
- 2 tablespoons chili powder
- 1½ teaspoons ground cumin
- 1½ teaspoons dried oregano
- ¾ teaspoon salt
- 3 cups corn chips
- 1 cup (4 ounces) shredded sharp Cheddar cheese
- 6 tablespoons chopped green onions

Jalapeño peppers can sting and irritate the skin, so wear rubber gloves when handling peppers and do not touch your eyes.

1. Coat inside of **CROCK-POT**® slow cooker with nonstick cooking spray.

2. Heat oil in large skillet over medium-high heat. Add onion, bell pepper, jalapeño pepper and garlic; cook and stir 2 minutes or until softened. Add beef; cook and stir 10 to 12 minutes or until beef is no longer pink and liquid has evaporated. Stir in green chiles; cook 1 minute. Remove beef mixture to **CROCK-POT**® slow cooker using slotted spoon. Stir in tomatoes, chili powder, cumin and oregano.

3. Cover; cook on LOW 6 to 7 hours or on HIGH 3½ to 4 hours. Stir in salt. Place corn chips evenly into serving bowls; top with chili. Sprinkle evenly with cheese and green onions.

BROCCOLI CHEDDAR SOUP

MAKES 6 SERVINGS

- 3 tablespoons butter
- 1 medium onion, chopped
- 3 tablespoons all-purpose flour
- ¼ teaspoon ground nutmeg
- ¼ teaspoon black pepper
- 4 cups vegetable broth
- 1 large bunch broccoli, chopped
- 1 medium red potato, peeled and chopped
- 1 teaspoon salt
- 1 whole bay leaf
- 1½ cups (6 ounces) shredded Cheddar cheese, plus additional for garnish
- ½ cup whipping cream

1. Melt butter in medium saucepan over medium heat. Add onion; cook and stir 6 minutes or until softened. Add flour, nutmeg and pepper; cook and stir 1 minute. Remove to **CROCK-POT**® slow cooker. Stir in broth, broccoli, potato, salt and bay leaf.

2. Cover; cook on HIGH 3 hours. Remove and discard bay leaf. Add soup in batches to food processor or blender; purée until desired consistency. Pour soup back into **CROCK-POT**® slow cooker. Stir in 1½ cups cheese and cream until cheese is melted. Garnish with additional cheese.

MEATBALLS AND SPAGHETTI SAUCE

MAKES 6 TO 8 SERVINGS

- 2 pounds ground beef
- 1 cup plain dry bread crumbs
- 1 onion, chopped
- 2 eggs, beaten
- ¼ cup minced fresh Italian parsley
- 4 teaspoons minced garlic, divided
- ½ teaspoon dry mustard
- ½ teaspoon black pepper
- 4 tablespoons olive oil, divided
- 1 can (28 ounces) whole tomatoes
- ½ cup chopped fresh basil
- 1 teaspoon sugar
- Salt and black pepper
- Hot cooked spaghetti

1. Combine beef, bread crumbs, onion, eggs, parsley, 2 teaspoons garlic, dry mustard and ½ teaspoon pepper in large bowl. Form into walnut-sized balls. Heat 2 tablespoons oil in large skillet over medium heat. Brown meatballs on all sides. Remove to **CROCK-POT**® slow cooker.

2. Combine tomatoes, basil, remaining 2 tablespoons oil, remaining 2 teaspoons garlic, sugar, salt and black pepper in medium bowl; stir to blend. Pour over meatballs, turn to coat. Cover; cook on LOW 3 to 5 hours or on HIGH 2 to 4 hours. Serve over spaghetti.

TIP: Recipe can be doubled for a 5-, 6- or 7-quart **CROCK-POT**® slow cooker.

SLOW-COOKED SHAKSHUKA

MAKES 6 SERVINGS

- ¼ cup extra virgin olive oil
- 1 medium onion, chopped
- 1 large red bell pepper, chopped
- 3 cloves garlic, sliced
- 1 can (28 ounces) crushed tomatoes with basil, garlic and oregano
- 2 teaspoons paprika
- 2 teaspoons ground cumin
- 2 teaspoons sugar
- ½ teaspoon salt
- ¼ teaspoon red pepper flakes
- ¾ cup crumbled feta cheese
- 6 eggs
- Chopped fresh cilantro (optional)
- Black pepper (optional)
- Toasted baguette slices (optional)

1. Coat inside of **CROCK-POT®** slow cooker with nonstick cooking spray. Combine oil, onion, bell pepper, garlic, tomatoes, paprika, cumin, sugar, salt and red pepper flakes in **CROCK-POT®** slow cooker; stir to blend. Cover; cook on HIGH 3 hours. Stir in feta cheese. Break eggs, one at a time, onto top of tomato mixture, leaving a little space between each.

2. Cover; cook on HIGH 15 to 18 minutes or until egg whites are set but yolks are still creamy. Scoop eggs and sauce evenly into each serving dish. Garnish with cilantro and black pepper. Serve with baguette slices, if desired.

HEARTY VEGETARIAN MAC AND CHEESE

MAKES 6 SERVINGS

- 1 can (about 14 ounces) stewed tomatoes, undrained
- 1½ cups prepared Alfredo sauce
- 1½ cups (6 ounces) shredded mozzarella cheese, divided
- 8 ounces whole grain pasta (medium shells or penne shape), cooked and drained
- 7 ounces Italian-flavored vegetarian sausage links, cut into ¼-inch slices
- ¾ cup fresh basil leaves, thinly sliced and divided
- ½ cup vegetable broth
- ½ teaspoon salt
- 2 tablespoons grated Parmesan cheese

1. Coat inside of **CROCK-POT**® slow cooker with nonstick cooking spray. Add tomatoes, Alfredo sauce, 1 cup mozzarella cheese, pasta, sausage, ½ cup basil, broth and salt to **CROCK-POT**® slow cooker; stir to blend. Top with remaining ½ cup mozzarella cheese and Parmesan cheese.

2. Cover; cook on LOW 3½ hours or on HIGH 2 hours. Top with remaining ¼ cup basil.

CHILE RELLEÑOS

MAKES 6 SERVINGS

- 6 whole poblano peppers
- 2½ cups (10 ounces) grated Chihuahua cheese or queso fresco, divided
- ½ cup plus 2 tablespoons prepared salsa verde, divided
- ¼ cup plus 2 tablespoons fresh cilantro leaves, divided
- 1 (1-inch) piece fresh serrano pepper
- 1 large clove garlic
- 1 can (12 ounces) evaporated milk
- 2 tablespoons all-purpose flour
- 2 eggs
- ⅔ cup sour cream

1. Coat inside of **CROCK-POT**® slow cooker with nonstick cooking spray. Place poblano peppers under broiler, about 4 inches from heat. Broil just until skins blister. Let cool slightly in large paper bag. Peel poblano peppers. Cut down one side of each poblano pepper; open flat to remove any seeds or membranes inside. Pat dry with paper towels.

2. Divide 1½ cups cheese evenly among poblano peppers; roll to enclose. Lay poblano peppers in single layer in bottom of **CROCK-POT**® slow cooker.

3. Combine ½ cup salsa verde, ¼ cup cilantro, serrano pepper and garlic in food processor or blender; pulse. Add milk, flour and eggs; process until smooth. Pour salsa mixture over poblano peppers; top with remaining 1 cup cheese. Cover; cook on LOW 3 hours.

4. Meanwhile, combine sour cream and remaining 2 tablespoons salsa verde in small bowl; stir to blend. Refrigerate sour cream mixture until ready to serve.

5. If desired, remove poblano peppers from **CROCK-POT**® slow cooker onto large baking sheet. Broil 3 to 5 minutes. Garnish with sour cream mixture and remaining 2 tablespoons cilantro.

STEAMED AFRICAN CORN LOAF

MAKES 8 SERVINGS

3 ears corn	½ cup cornmeal
2 eggs	1 tablespoon sugar
2 tablespoons melted butter	2 teaspoons baking powder
½ cup all-purpose flour	½ teaspoon salt

1. Spray 7×4-inch loaf pan that fits inside of oval **CROCK-POT**® slow cooker with nonstick cooking spray. Cut kernels from corn; measure 1½ cups. Combine 1 cup corn, eggs and butter in food processor or blender; pulse until well mixed (not smooth). Add remaining ½ cup corn; pulse briefly (some corn should remain whole).

2. Combine flour, cornmeal, sugar, baking powder and salt in medium bowl; stir to blend. Add corn mixture; stir until dry ingredients are just moistened. *Do not overmix.* Spoon batter evenly into prepared pan. Cut one 14-inch piece foil; fold in half. Place foil on top of pan, crimping very tightly around edges. Place pan in **CROCK-POT**® slow cooker. Add 1 inch of water around sides of pan.

3. Cover; cook on HIGH 4 to 4½ hours. Remove pan from **CROCK-POT**® slow cooker; remove foil. Cut around loaf with knife to loosen; flip pan over onto wire rack. Cool bread 10 minutes; flip loaf over before slicing.

COLCANNON

MAKES 8 SERVINGS

- 6 tablespoons butter, cut into small pieces
- 3 pounds russet potatoes, peeled and cut into 1-inch pieces
- 2 medium leeks, white and light green parts only, thinly sliced
- ½ cup water
- 2½ teaspoons kosher salt
- ¼ teaspoon black pepper
- 1 cup milk
- ½ small head (about 1 pound) savoy cabbage, cored and thinly sliced
- 4 slices bacon, crisp-cooked and crumbled

1. Sprinkle butter on bottom of **CROCK-POT**® slow cooker. Layer half of potatoes, leeks, remaining potatoes, water, salt and pepper. Cover; cook on HIGH 5 hours or until potatoes are tender, stirring halfway through cooking time.

2. Mash potatoes in **CROCK-POT**® slow cooker until smooth. Stir in milk and cabbage. Cover; cook on HIGH 30 to 40 minutes or until cabbage is crisp-tender. Stir bacon into potato mixture.

TWICE "BAKED" POTATOES

MAKES 4 SERVINGS

- 4 baking potatoes (about 10 ounces *each*)
- 3 tablespoons olive oil, divided
- 1 head garlic
- 1 to 2 tablespoons milk
- 4 tablespoons sour cream
- ½ teaspoon salt
- ¼ teaspoon black pepper
- 2 slices bacon, cooked and chopped
- ½ cup (2 ounces) shredded Cheddar cheese, divided
- ¼ teaspoon smoked paprika
- Chopped green onions (optional)

1. Rub potatoes with 2 tablespoons oil; wrap each potato in foil. Place potatoes in **CROCK-POT®** slow cooker. Cut across top of garlic head. Place garlic in foil; top with remaining 1 tablespoon oil. Twist foil closed around garlic; place on top of potatoes. Cover; cook on HIGH 4 hours or until potatoes are soft when pierced with knife.

2. Pull foil away from each potato; crimp it around bottom of potatoes. Cut thin slice from top of each potato. Scoop inside of potatoes into large bowl, leaving about ¼-inch shell. Squeeze garlic head to remove softened cloves; mash with fork. Measure 1 tablespoon mashed garlic; add to large bowl with potatoes. Refrigerate remaining garlic in airtight jar for another use.

3. Add milk, sour cream, salt and pepper to large bowl with potatoes; beat with electric mixer at medium speed 3 to 4 minutes or until smooth. Stir in bacon and half of cheese. Spoon mashed potatoes into shells, mounding at top. Top with remaining cheese and paprika. Return potatoes to **CROCK-POT®** slow cooker. Cover; cook on HIGH 15 minutes or until cheese is melted. Garnish with green onions.

ROCKY ROAD BROWNIE BOTTOMS

MAKES 6 SERVINGS

- ½ cup packed brown sugar
- ½ cup water
- 2 tablespoons unsweetened cocoa powder
- 2½ cups packaged brownie mix
- 1 package (about 4 ounces) instant chocolate pudding mix
- ½ cup milk chocolate chips
- 2 eggs, beaten
- 3 tablespoons butter, melted
- 2 cups mini marshmallows
- 1 cup chopped pecans or walnuts, toasted*
- ½ cup chocolate syrup

To toast pecans, spread in single layer in heavy skillet. Cook and stir over medium heat 1 to 2 minutes or until nuts are lightly browned.

1. Prepare foil handles by tearing off three 18×2-inch strips heavy foil (or use regular foil folded to double thickness). Crisscross foil strips in spoke design; place in **CROCK-POT®** slow cooker. Coat inside of **CROCK-POT®** slow cooker with nonstick cooking spray.

2. Combine brown sugar, water and cocoa in small saucepan over medium heat; bring to a boil over medium-high heat. Meanwhile, combine brownie mix, pudding mix, chocolate chips, eggs and butter in medium bowl; stir until well blended. Spread batter in **CROCK-POT®** slow cooker; pour boiling sugar mixture over batter.

3. Cover; cook on HIGH 1½ hours. Turn off heat. Top brownies with marshmallows, pecans and chocolate syrup. Let stand 15 minutes. Use foil handles to lift brownie to serving platter.

NOTE: Recipe can be doubled for a 5-, 6- or 7-quart **CROCK-POT®** slow cooker.

CINNAMON ROLL-TOPPED MIXED BERRY COBBLER

MAKES 8 SERVINGS

- 2 bags (12 ounces *each*) frozen mixed berries, thawed
- 1 cup sugar
- ¼ cup quick-cooking tapioca
- ¼ cup water
- 2 teaspoons vanilla
- 1 package (about 12 ounces) refrigerated cinnamon rolls with icing

Combine berries, sugar, tapioca, water and vanilla in **CROCK-POT®** slow cooker; top with cinnamon rolls. Cover; cook on LOW 4 to 5 hours. Serve warm, drizzled with icing.

NOTE: This recipe was designed to work best in a 4-quart **CROCK-POT®** slow cooker. Double the ingredients for larger **CROCK-POT®** slow cookers, but always place cinnamon rolls in a single layer.